# FIT FOR THE GAME
# RUGBY

## Jim Golby

WARD LOCK

Designed and produced by SP Creative Design
St Andrews House, 33 St Andrews Street South
Bury St Edmunds, Suffolk

Editor: Heather Thomas
Art Director: Rolando Ugolini

Text set in Univers medium by Halcyon Type & Design Ltd, Ipswich
Printed and bound in Great Britain by Richard Clay Ltd.

British Library Cataloguing in Publication Data

Golby, Jim
  Rugby.
  1. Sports. Health
  I. Title II. Series
  613.711

ISBN 0-7063-6934-3

# Jim Golby

Jim Golby is Senior Lecturer in the Faculty of Cultural and Educational Studies at Leeds Polytechnic. He has wide experience in coaching rugby teams and running weight-training and fitness courses, and is Staff Tutor to the National Coaching Foundation.

He was a Rugby League and Amateur Athletic coach and a National Cricket Association Staff Coach, and is a Life Member of the British Amateur Weight Lifting Association. He has acted as a consultant to St Helen's Rugby League Club, Bradford and Bingley Rugby Union Football Club, Yorkshire County Cricket Club, Northants County Cricket Club, Hull Kingston Rovers Rugby League Football Club and the All England Netball Association.

He now acts as consultant on training matters to Cambridge University Rugby Union Football Club. He is a visiting lecturer to numerous sports bodies and associations. Dr Golby is married with one son.

## Acknowledgements

The author would like to thank everybody who helped him on this book, especially Andy Clarke, Andreas Liefeith and Martin Pepper for their assistance in the production of the photographs.

The publishers would like to thank Leeds Polytechnic for their assistance and use of their facilities.

All the photographs are courtesy of Mark Shearman with the exception of the cover photograph and photographs on pages 6 and 11, which were supplied by Russell Cheyne, AllSport.

# CONTENTS

# CHAPTER ONE

# PLANNING FITNESS TRAINING

A number of key questions are asked by every coach and player involved in rugby football. They repeatedly wish to know how best to train for rugby, what exercises to do and how hard should these exercises be done. They also ask when should such training best take place.

The chapters in this book will give a detailed account of how all rugby players can develop aerobic and anaerobic fitness, power and strength, as well as mobility. Thus it will guide the club coach as well as the individual player who wants to take responsibility for his fitness preparation. However, it is important that the development of these aspects of fitness is placed within the framework of a proper training plan.

To answer these fundamental questions correctly, it is very important that the coach or individual player has a carefully constructed and realistic strategy. Without adequate planning, training and coaching are often reduced to the level of random events, lacking both purpose and development.

The plan should include a detailed outline of the preparation of the team over the course of a season. This will, of course, include details of close season activities. It should also state the aims and objectives of

*Mike Teague is an International player who has built up his strength with a well constructed fitness programme.*

each single team session and those of every squad member taking part in that particular session.

Effective planning has two very important functions: it sets attainable targets towards which players can work; and it spells out a clear step-by-step method of working towards such targets. Indeed, it is true to say that 'winning is the science of correct preparation'.

Being prepared applies as much to the appropriate physical conditioning of players as it does to the selection and application of the appropriate techniques, skills, strategies and tactics.

Before looking at the specific details of planning a fitness training programme, three general considerations are important in the overall planning of the physical preparation for rugby. The first of these is the elements of which rugby is composed. The second consideration is the specific physiological demands of the positions occupied by the players in a team. These two important pieces of information need also to be considered alongside a third, which involves a set of general principles on which all training is based.

## The elements of performing in rugby

It is impossible to discuss the concept of fitness and its evaluation without first of all outlining what is meant by the term 'fitness' and why it is important to measure and assess it. A lot of players get confused about what really constitutes fitness, and most of this stems from an understandable desire to make a definition apply to everything under the sun: health, economic success and happiness. If someone was to ask, 'Are you fit?', how would you reply?

Perhaps the best way round this problem is to say that it is impossible to discuss fitness unless you use the word 'for' in conjunction with the word 'fitness'. A person is 'fit for' something; indeed it is generally accepted that a person who is physically fit in every respect does not and probably cannot exist.

A champion marathon runner might be regarded by most of us as being fit, but how would he shape up in the front row of a rugby scrum? A teacher of physical education is, or should be, seen by his colleagues as being fit, but how does he shape up after a day of scrubbing floors or minding a baby?

Fitness then is relative to the task at hand, and in order to develop it we need to break it down into some of its components and then to assess them.

When designing a training programme, it is important to consider the six 'S' factors. These consist of:

- Speed
- Strength (static and power)
- Stamina (endurance)
- Suppleness (mobility)
- Skill
- pSychology

Clearly, since all of these factors have a place in rugby performance, the coach or the individual player will wish to make improvements in any or all of these. It has, however, become abundantly clear that it is a fruitless exercise to hold either a single

training session or a block of sessions in which every member of a squad follows the same selection of activities at the same intensity. Emphasis will vary according to the time of year, position in the team and the condition of the individual. There is, therefore, no such thing as an ideal schedule which will meet the needs of all players. Certainly everybody will need to attain good general levels of the factors listed above but in varying degrees. Match analysis has revealed different physiological demands on different playing positions. The findings can be used to group players for training purposes.

## Grouping of players for training purposes

This is a classification that is very useful in schedule construction. Although it is based on Rugby Union it exemplifies a methodology that can be applied to other forms of rugby football.

### Group A

One group of players are the **props** and the **locks**. Players in both of these positions have a continuous level of involvement in the game which requires a high level of aerobic capacity. They are also involved in close physical exchanges which demand high levels of power (i.e scrummage, ruck and maul).

### Group B

Consists of **back row forwards, hookers** and the **half backs**. These players have a more spasmodic pattern of play which is characterized by sudden highly explosive activity.

### Group C

This group consists of **full backs, wings** and **centres**. Their pattern of play, in the main, consists of short periods of high speed and powerful running with the occasional period of physical contact demanding strength and power.

Once the elements on which performance in rugby is based have been considered, and the specific demands of each position examined, it is important to examine some basic principles that apply to all physical training.

## Principles of training

### Specificity

It is crucial to note that the adaptation to training is highly specific. For example, to improve power, a player must work on strengthening; and to improve stamina, endurance work must be done.

### Progression

In order to ensure that improvement continues to be made, schedules need to be reviewed and amended as the capacity of the player increases. There should be a gradual increase in the quantity and/or the quality of work depending on the position in the training cycle.

### Reversibility

When a lessening of the training load occurs or, as when the player is injured, it ceases altogether, the fitness level will start to decline. It is a useful guide to remember that 'slow gain' training methods suffer a slower decline than do the 'fast gain' methods.

### Overload

The coach should ensure that the activity being performed must exceed in intensity or duration the regular performance demands encountered by the player.

### Assessment

Research evidence has shown that feedback, in the form of the measurement of performance, is essential if the player is to respond positively to the targets set by the coach.

The final two factors in devising a successful plan for the player and club involve the coach in utilizing two important divisions: firstly, the phasing of the rugby year into relevant sections, each with its own aims and objectives; and secondly, the specific training requirements of the three groups of players previously identified.

## Phases of the rugby year

It is useful in planning if the coach can make two important divisions. The first of these is the splitting of the rugby year into three distinct phases, each with its own special contribution to the overall goal. The second split, which will be discussed later in this chapter, involves the dividing of the players into distinct groups for training purposes.

The splitting of the rugby year or **periodization** helps in preparing players to peak at the correct time as well as allowing them to achieve a steady growth and development in physical attributes over the course of a normal playing career.

The term **macrocycle** can be used to describe these big cycles of the training year. Each of these may, in turn, be composed of a number of **microcycles** of, for example, seven, ten or fourteen days duration.

The **close-season** phase is when the player attempts to develop and build up the bedrock of physical qualities demanded by his role in the game. This period follows a term of 'active recovery' during which he takes part in other non-game related activities in order to help him rebuild his mental condition, allow his body to recuperate and to recharge his appetite for the game. It is in this phase that strength and endurance in particular are developed.

As this period draws to a close, about eight weeks prior to the commencement of the first competitive game, the **pre-season** phase is entered. Thus, as the stamina or endurance work is reduced, so speed and power work are increased. It is at this stage that more of the game-related fitness activities are included.

The goal of the third and final phase, the **competitive** phase, is the maintenance of the appropriate levels of fitness required to perform at maximal level.

It is worth pointing out that the quantity of the close-season training gradually gives way to the quality of the competitive phase.

The transition from the first to the final of the macrocycles can be seen as a shift from **preparation** to **adaptation** and on to **application** or a shift from general conditioning to specific conditioning.

When working out the small details of an individual's programme, adequate time must be allowed for rest and recovery if injury or staleness are to be avoided. Further to this aim, the coach should ensure that the training is varied and interesting, and that the players enjoy the sessions as much as possible.

Before giving a practical example of how these principles are applied to planning a specific schedule, it is important to examine in greater detail the specific physiological demands placed on players occupying different positions since this will clearly affect schedule construction.

## Training needs of specific playing groups

**Group A** (props and locks)
Because of their continuous involvement with the game this group of players requires a high level of aerobic fitness. Thus training would initially concentrate on increasing the ability of their body to use oxygen ($VO_2$ max.) as well as the creation of the correct lean body mass/fat ratio if necessary.

This group also needs to work on their anaerobic fitness for such activities as the snap shove in the scrum or leaping in the line-outs as well as the occasions when they find themselves with the ball in their hands.

Since strength is a necessary prerequisite for increased power, Group A will concentrate on strength when working on their first macrocycle which includes their early aerobic work. In the Northern Hemisphere this would be in May, June and early July. The switch to power training is best done with the switch to the second macrocycle which focuses on anaerobic work. This would be in late July and August.

**Group B** (back row forwards, hookers and half backs)
Players in this group of positions are required to produce an intermittent type of running which is characterized by a number of explosive bursts. The first macrocycle of these players will be similar in content to that of the Group A players. However, when the coach feels that the appropriate level of aerobic fitness has been gained, an earlier shift to, say, interval running (or some other form of intermittent running) would be appropriate.

All players need to develop the anaerobic lactic area, but groups B and C need

*Rob Andrew is an England International who has developed speed and flexibility with the help of a well balanced training programme.*

to develop the anaerobic alactic area too, which is involved in speed.

A strength/power programme would suit this group with the transition as for group A.

**Group C** (full backs, wings and centres)
From a sound basis of aerobic fitness, which would enable a speedy repayment of any oxygen debt incurred, these players will focus rather more on the development and maintenance of speed. They will also need upper body strength and leg power without undue bulk. This will be achieved by the use of a correct weight-training programme and the use of plyometric exercises.

It is now felt that while strength development enhances speed potential, it is insufficient to guarantee speed of execution of an activity. Thus this group needs to include speed drills and specific forms of training.

Listed below is a sample schedule based on the principles of planning a fitness training programme outlined in this chapter.

## Sample schedule for a Group A player

**Close season phase (6 - 8 weeks)**
In order to maintain correct body composition, to improve aerobic performance and to develop strength, players in this group should work on something like the activities listed below:
**Aerobic:** run 3 times a week for 40 mins (or equivalent) or light circuits with heart rate 160-165 using body resistance.
**Flexibility:** daily session of flexibility exercises.
**Strength:** 3 sessions per week at 70-80% max. weights, 3-4 sets of 4-6 reps., good recovery between exercises.

**Pre-season phase (6 - 8 weeks)**
To continue improving aerobic capacity and to work towards harnessing strength into power, this group of players could do the following programme:
**Aerobic:** continue with circuits 3 times a week or 3 hard 30-minute runs per week.
**Anaerobic:** work is introduced in this session – bounding exercises or fast hopping on one leg over 20m, 3 sets of 6 each leg. Four sets of 5 x 30m sprints.
**Strength/power:** 3 sessions per week. Shift to 70% maximum lift performed at speed. Sets of 6-8. Introduce power exercises such as power clean, jerk from racks, Neider press to replace slower exercises.
**Flexibility:** daily programme of exercises.

**In-season phase**
The aim of this phase is to maintain all levels and to enable the player to play well in matches. For example:
**Aerobic:** a recovery run on the day following a match is a useful way of alleviating soreness and maintaining aerobic fitness. In addition, 2 brisk/fast-pace 30-minute runs help maintain this aspect of fitness.
**Anaerobic:** 2 speed sessions each week during this phase. Plyometrics can be included as well as working with a ball.
**Strength/power:** 1 session per week as for pre-season phase.
**Flexibility:** as per each phase.

# CHAPTER TWO

# DEVELOPING AEROBIC ENDURANCE

It is difficult, if not impossible, for coaches or players to gain sufficient knowledge of how to develop winning fitness without understanding something of how the body functions. Whilst this, of necessity, involves the use of some of the jargon employed by the exercise physiologist, what follows need not deter you since detailed biochemistry will, wherever possible, be avoided. However, it is important that prior to examining ways of improving specific aspects of fitness, some explanation of how that particular system operates is essential. Coaches and players are encouraged to come to grips with basic physiology prior to planning a training schedule.

## What is endurance?

The use of the term 'endurance' does not really help the coach in planning schedules since it is an extremely broad term. It could be used to describe the last 15 minutes of a game or the last 80 metres of a 400 metres run put in by a flanker during a particularly long play-phase. Thus 'endurance' covers a wide range of activities lasting from seconds to days (as in, for example, World Cup competitions).

One useful way of splitting down the concept of endurance is to divide it into 'long-term' and 'short-term'. It is usual to take the divide at one minute, thus 'short-term' refers to events of less than 60 seconds in duration (anaerobic endurance), and events of over 60 seconds are concerned with 'long-term', or aerobic, endurance.

## Aerobic endurance

Long-term endurance, often called stamina by older players, really refers to aerobic endurance. The term 'aerobic' is best described by its literal meaning: 'with air'. Aerobic endurance suggests muscular work which uses oxygen to free energy from the muscle fuels. A division of the aerobic system into the cardio-respiratory system, which is responsible for transporting oxygen to the muscles, and for the utilization of that oxygen inside each muscle cell at the local level, is a useful way of looking at aerobic endurance. It is obvious that there is little value in possessing a marvellously efficient network for providing the muscles with oxygen if the muscle is not in the correct condition to utilize it. It may help the coach and those on the coaching team responsible for the fitness of players if they have some understanding of the oxygen transport system and its utilization.

## Cardio-respiratory system

In total this system is composed of the lungs, heart, blood vessels and the blood they contain.

**13**

# DEVELOPING AEROBIC ENDURANCE

## The lungs

During heavy exercise something in the order of 150-200 litres of air can be breathed in one minute as opposed to the 10 or so litres breathed at rest. Once in the lungs the gases pass down the air tubes which divide into smaller and smaller branches until they reach the air sacs, called alveoli, where the oxygen diffuses across the wall of the air sacs into the capillary blood vessels behind them.

Carbon dioxide, which is returning from the working muscles, makes the opposite journey and is subsequently breathed out. Research tends to suggest that, even with intensive aerobic training over a period, little change occurs in the lungs. It could be that an increase in the strength of those muscles responsible for respiration results in an increase of about 10 per cent in their capacity. However, what does improve with training is not so much an improvement in getting the oxygen but an improvement in transporting it. It is the heart that is responsible for this action.

## The heart

Once again there is a large difference between resting values and values taken during heavy exercise in terms of the performance of the heart. At rest the heart pumps around five litres of blood whereas during strenuous physical activity this may increase to about 30 or more litres in a well-conditioned rugby player. This increase is made possible by a rise in heart rate from around 70 beats per minute (depending on age and physical condition) to about 200 beats per minute. There is also an increase in stroke volume (blood pumped at each beat) from a resting level of about 85ml of blood to an exercise level of 130ml.

As a consequence of training, the maximum heart rate does not increase but stroke volume does, whether at rest or during exercise. Training brings about an increase in the size, strength and thickness of the heart muscle. The chambers of the heart also show an increase in volume.

## The blood vessels

Taken together, all the blood vessels are known as the 'vascular system'. This includes those vessels that take blood to the muscles, i.e. arteries, and those that carry blood away from the muscles back to the heart, i.e. veins.

At the level of the cell itself are the smallest blood vessels of all, the capillaries. At this level the actual gaseous exchanges themselves take place. These consist of oxygen diffusing out and carbon dioxide diffusing back, as well as the two muscle fuels of blood glucose and free fatty acids diffusing out. At this level also, the hormone insulin diffuses out to the muscle cell and lactic acid may, to be removed, diffuse from the muscle into the blood. Thus the capillaries are the focal point of the whole system.

When beginning exercise, you encounter the 'vascular shunt', or the re-routing of the blood, to provide the muscles with an increase in blood. Whereas at rest about 40 per cent of the heart's output goes to the liver and kidneys, when exercise starts, this is reduced to about 10 per cent of its original value. Blood is also re-routed from the abdomen and pelvic organs and the skin.

As your level of fitness increases, little happens to the shunt, but the number of capillary blood vessels in the muscle increase – a phenomenon that also seems to occur in the heart.

### The blood

The normal male rugby player will have around a gallon of blood circulating in his system. Of this blood about 20 per cent is located in the arteries at any one time and the remaining 80 per cent in the veins. In terms of aerobic endurance perhaps the most important measure is the amount of haemoglobin in the blood. Haemoglobin is the chemical located in the red cells of the blood and is responsible for carrying 99 per cent of the oxygen. In the normal male, the range of haemoglobin is between 14 and 16 grams for every 100ml of blood. If the haemoglobins are less than these figures then the player may be suffering from some *anaemia*. The situation is complicated when you consider that in a number of very fit endurance sports people, one of the results of their endurance training has been an increase in the amount of blood in the body. This hypervolaemia may involve increases of up to 50 per cent, but it is notable that the red cells do not quite match the plasma (fluid) increase, so that although there is much more blood, and consequently more haemoglobin in total, the real concentration of red cells and their haemoglobin is effectively less.

## Assessment of aerobic capacity

When planning a fitness training programme, it is useful for both the coach and the players to monitor the aerobic fitness of everyone in the squad. Some form of step-up test is of value in checking on progress and making the necessary adjustments to the schedules since it is designed to estimate the body's capacity to adjust and recover from hard muscular work.

Once levels are deemed to be satisfactory, the emphasis in training can then shift to maintaining aerobic performance and, consequently, placing emphasis on the other aspects of fitness.

## Training for aerobic endurance

By now it will be clear that the heart is the target organ as far as physical preparation is concerned; partly because it shows the greatest response but also because it is fairly easily measured. The purpose of aerobic endurance training is to elevate the heart rate to an appropriate level and to maintain this level for the correct period of time. The problem for the coach lies in deciding what is an appropriate level and how long a heart rate should be maintained at such a level. For a young player in his twenties, perhaps three half-hourly training sessions a week at the appropriate time in the calendar at a heart rate of around 150 beats per minute will produce a significant increase in aerobic fitness. The better conditioned you are, the harder you need to work. Effectively, this means stepping up both the frequency of sessions, their length and their severity.

A working guide to top-performance training is to add 25 to your age and subtract that from a total of 220 to give an approximate training pulse rate. For example, a 25-year-old player would have a training pulse of 170 beats per minute.

The most effective form of training for improving your central oxygen transport system is continuous running involving as large a muscle mass as possible.

For the specific purposes of rugby, the maximum running time need only be 30-40 minutes since any time longer than this will be better suited to long distance running or marathon training and render you vulnerable to the type of injuries encountered by runners. Indeed, it may be better for the big men in the team to consider cycling or swimming as an alternative to running for long periods on hard surfaces. Experience teaches us that the players wishing to cycle should multiply their running distance by three, and if they wish to swim, they should divide it by four. At any rate aerobic work is best prescribed in accordance with your particular preference. In all cases, you should work with the heart operating in the target zone.

## Use of circuits in aerobic training

Circuits are a suitable form of aerobic training which could be offered as an alternative to running. They are beneficial in motivating players and can be performed indoors, a valuable asset in the British climate. Additionally they have some beneficial effects on strength conditioning.

The quantity of work is increased as performance improves and thus the 'roof' of aerobic capacity is lifted. This phenomenon is described as the **anaerobic threshold**.

Circuit training involves the completion of a certain number of exercises within a limited time. Within this framework there are a number of variations. In most cases, however, the apparatus used is spaced around the training facility and there is usually a card illustrating each exercise and indicating the correct performance. One form of circuit is where you start on the 'easy' circuit, identified by the cards, and complete the requisite number of repetitions (eg. 10 sit-ups, 12 jump-chins etc.) before completing the circuit three times.

As soon as this circuit can be completed in less than a set time you progress to the circuit identified as of 'medium' intensity and subsequently to the 'hard' circuit.

Perhaps a more valuable *individual* approach is offered by the second form of training session where at the first session you are tested to maximum on each activity. This is done either by repetitions of the exercise to exhaustion, or the maximum achievable in one minute. A one-minute period of rest is allowed before testing the next exercise. For subsequent sessions the work dosage will then be set at 50 per cent of the initial score achieved, and you will complete three laps of the circuit as quickly as possible and your time will be recorded. After four to six weeks, re-testing can take place and new work loads are set.

A third form of circuit is one in which the coach has all players working maximally on a particular activity for some target time (say, 30 seconds). A brief rest follows before all players move on to the next exercise in the circuit.

It is, of course, possible to devise specific rugby exercises to feature in all or part of the circuit in order to help the specific preparation of players.

## Example of a general aerobic fitness circuit

The circuit on page 24 is suitable for any player working on aerobic fitness and has the benefit of being easy to set up and administer. This is often important since, unfortunately, specialist facilities are not always immediately available. If the player is working alone, not much space is required. However, if a group of players are working out, it is important that exercises are well spaced out in order to avoid impeding each other or causing injury.

## Assessment

The player should be tested to discover the maximum number of repetitions he can complete in 60 seconds. Note that, if necessary, the player may rest and then continue exercising within the 60-second period. You should allow 2 minutes rest between each exercise.

When the circuit has been completed, each score is recorded and on the next occasion that circuit training is scheduled, the player should bring his individual work card with him. This card will show the name of each exercise and the number of repetitions to be completed on that exercise. This is simply half the maximum completed in the 60 seconds of work done on the assessment day. The player will then complete 3 circuits with little or no rest between the 3 x 10 exercises. In other words, the player performs the half-maximum scores on exercises 1-10 and repeats this another time before stopping. The aim is to work through the exercises, using the correct technique, as quickly as possible and to record the time taken. As a rough guide, the three circuits should be completed in just under 30 minutes. Once the player can complete the circuits in under 20 minutes, he should be re-tested on the next visit.

Before embarking on any training activities it is important to remember that all good fitness sessions should have an enjoyable beginning, a demanding middle section and a pleasant warm-down. Both coaches and individual players should come to the training session with a prepared plan. Like all plans, however, it may need to be flexible since people, unlike most machines, do not operate in the same way on every occasion. For example, if you are over-tired, distracted or even feeling in particularly good shape, modifications may be necessary.

## Warm-up session

All sessions should begin with an adequate warm-up designed to stretch muscles. Since it is important that cold muscles should not be stretched, a slow jog lasting for about 5 minutes which starts to induce light perspiration should precede stretching exercises. It is important not to 'pump' or move the frame during stretching.

**Important points to remember**

● **Be careful:** stretching should be applied slowly.

● **Be methodical:** complete each stretch before moving on to the next.

● **Be uncompetitive:** ignore the ability of others since your body is unique.

● **Be observant:** monitor your improvement.

● **Be regular:** maintain the stretching habit, and do this before all training sessions and all games.

# Warm-up exercises

## Abdominal twist

**1** Lie on your back on the ground. Place your fingers on the sides of your head and pull the knees upward to the chest, raising your head towards the knees into the start-ing cradle position.

**2** Use the right elbow to touch the left knee, then the left elbow to the right knee. Alternate as fast as possible. Repeat 30 times.

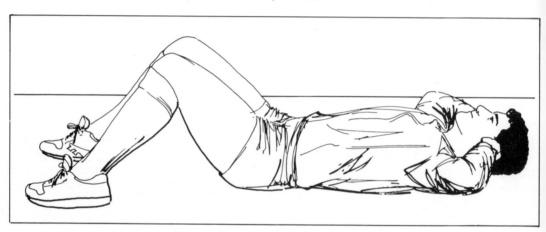

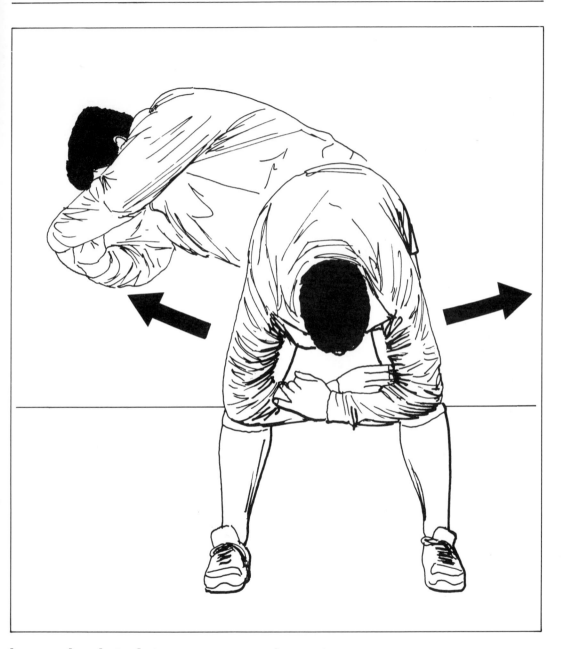

## Lower back twist

**1** With legs just wider than shoulder width apart, bend forward at the waist. Keeping the forearms parallel to the ground, bend the arms at the elbow.

**2** Rotate the trunk from left to right with a sweeping motion forcefully stretching the lower back. Repeat 30 times.

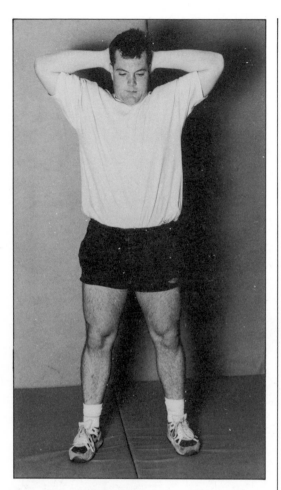

## Trunk rotation

**1** With feet shoulder width apart, bend your knees slightly and interlock your fingers behind your neck.

**2** Bend from the waist and touch the right elbow to the right knee.

**3** Rotate the trunk to the right and then bend backwards, forcing the hips forwards, and continue rotating the trunk to touch the left elbow to the left knee.

**4** Continue rotating to the starting position, bending forwards with both elbows touching both knees.

## Hamstring stretches

**1** Stand upright and cross one foot over the other with the heel of the crossed leg up, thus keeping the pelvis straight.

**2** On a slow 1-2 count, reach down towards the ground, and, on a count of three, touch the ground. Repeat this 10 times, then cross the other leg and repeat 10 times.

## Quadriceps stretches

**1** Kneel and point the toes away from the body behind you.

**2** Lean backwards and place your hands on the arches of your feet, at the same time lifting the pelvis up and out. You should feel the stretch in the quadriceps. Repeat 20 times.

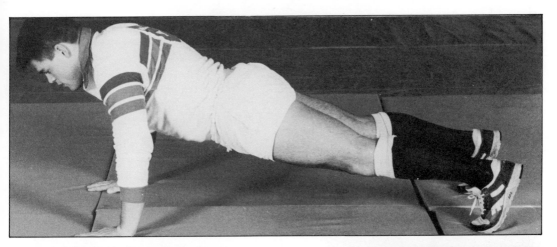

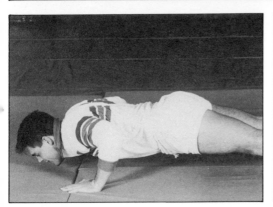

## Circular push-up

**1** Assume the press-up position.

**2** Lower your shoulders towards the floor at the same time arching your body.

**3** Then drive your body forwards into the lower press-up position. Repeat 10 times.

## General circuit exercises

### Press-ups

**1** Lie face downwards and raise your body off the ground supporting it with your arms, palms flat on the floor.

**2** Lower your chest towards the floor, keeping your back straight. Raise your body slowly off the floor again.

## Squat jumps

**1** Squat down in the starting position with one foot slightly in front of the other. Keep your head upright and touch the floor with the fingertips of both hands.

**2** With an explosive leap, jump up, changing your feet in mid-air. Land with the feet reversed and then repeat.

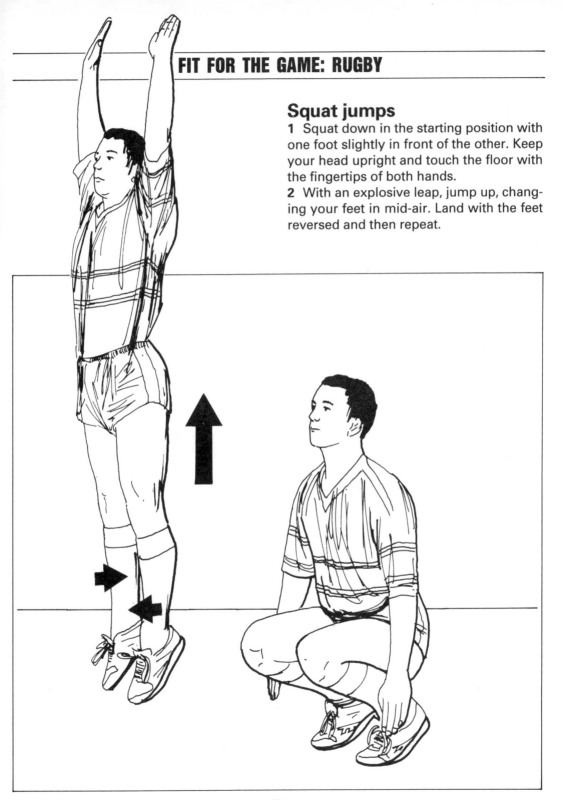

## Trunk twists

**1** Lie on the floor with knees bent and feet under a bar. With your head and shoulders raised off the ground, place the palms of your hands on either side of your head.

**2** Sit up and twist to the left so that the right elbow touches the left knee. Repeat, twisting to the other side.

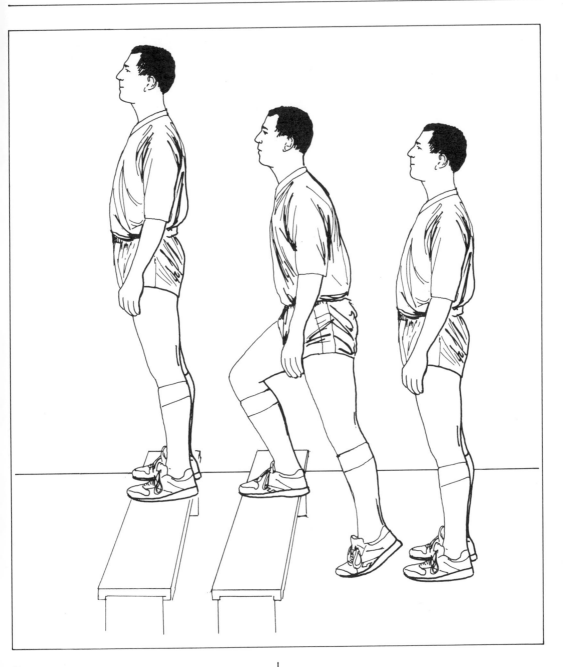

## Step-ups

**1** Stand in front of a bench with back straight, eyes looking straight ahead.

**2** Step up on to the bench and then step down again. Repeat, changing legs.

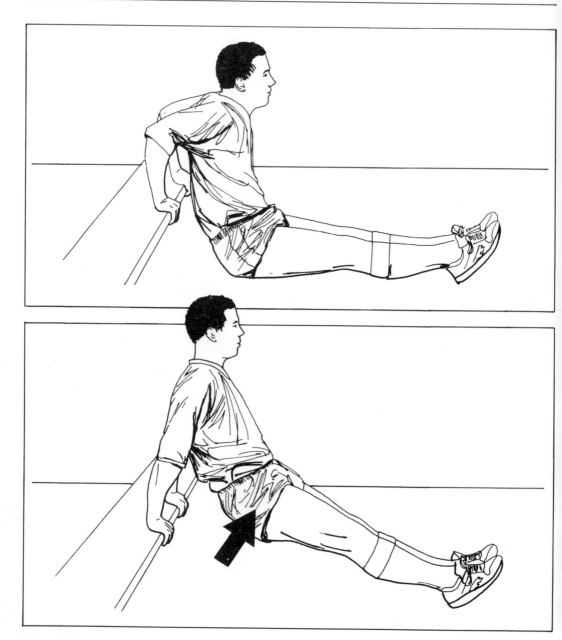

## Modified dips

**1** Sit with your legs outstretched and weight on the heels, with elbows bent and hands resting on the bench behind you.

**2** Extend your arms to lock them behind you and raise your body off the ground. Slowly lower your body back to the ground.

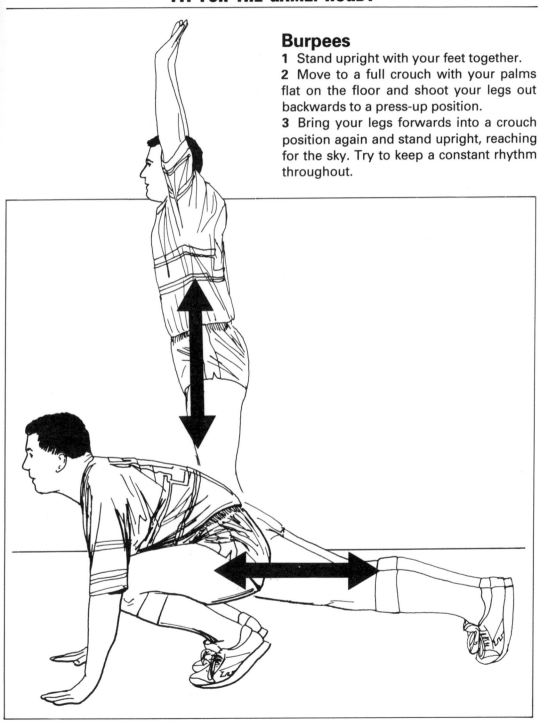

## Burpees

**1** Stand upright with your feet together.

**2** Move to a full crouch with your palms flat on the floor and shoot your legs out backwards to a press-up position.

**3** Bring your legs forwards into a crouch position again and stand upright, reaching for the sky. Try to keep a constant rhythm throughout.

## Back raises *above*

1 Lie face downwards across a bench with a partner holding your feet on the floor.
2 Simultaneously lift the head and upper body into the air, keeping your hands behind your head. Lower slowly under control.

## Shuttle runs

Sprint as quickly as possible between two designated markers.

## Astride jumps

1 Stand on the floor with your legs astride a bench or solid box.
2 Jump up to land on the bench with feet together. Jump down on the floor again. You can increase the work-load by jumping with a medicine ball or dumbbells.

# Examples of rugby-specific circuit exercises

Once a general level of fitness has been achieved, it may be advantageous, for motivational as well as for physiological reasons, to progress to a circuit more specifically tailored towards helping the player to adapt to the particular demands of rugby. Listed below is an example of such a circuit.

## Shuttle run

**1** Carrying a rugby ball in both hands, sprint from a starting line to a line 5m away.
**2** Touch it with the ball and run back to the starting line.
**3** Without rest run back to a line 10m away and back again.
**4** Then repeat the exercise, running to a line 15m away and back. Each line is touched with the ball. Either maximum number in a certain time or alternating with a partner is possible.

## Scrummage

Two players engage in a one-man scrummage for a set period of time, then disengage and walk back to the starting mark.

## Scrum half pass

1 A number of balls are placed on a line.
2 A player passes to a partner or target, then runs to a mark 5m away and back to pass a second ball and so on.

## Side step

1 Place 4 cones on a line.
2 Run forwards and side-step the cones in order.
3 Turn at the last one and repeat, going back to the starting point.

## Passing

Two partners move up and down a 20m channel inter-passing a ball.

## Leg thrust *below*

1 One player adopts a starting position lying on his back with legs raised and held out straight.
2 Another player presses his knees and hips into full flexion.
3 The player on his back then straightens his legs against his partner's resistance.

## Pick-up on run

**1** Both players stand on the starting line with player A holding the ball.

**2** Player A rolls the ball to B for him to sprint and collect.

**3** When B returns to the starting line, both players then sprint to a second line 10m away and the drill is repeated with roles reversed.

## Tackling on mats

**1** Player A holds a tackle bag in the middle of a well-covered area.

**2** Player B runs from 3m to tackle the bag.

**3** The players can either exchange roles and alternate between holding or tackling the bag, or Player A can continue for a certain period of time or a given number of repetitions.

## Box rebound

**1** Player A stands on a box holding a ball out in front of him as high as possible.

**2** Player B jumps to take the ball, lands, then jumps to return the ball to A on the box. The players change halfway through the drill.

# CHAPTER THREE

# DEVELOPING ANAEROBIC ENDURANCE

As we have seen, when planning a physical conditioning programme for a rugby player you need to consider the following factors:

● His immediate physical status at the outset of the regimen.
● The function demanded of him by the team's playing policy.
● The qualities demanded for successful fulfilment of your immediate positional role (e.g. full back, prop etc.).

All players need the ability to meet the various physical demands of the game at the level at which they play. This ability, as we have noted, is often termed **endurance**.

In the previous chapter, we looked at the development of long-term endurance, i.e. continuous exercise for over one minute. This split of exercise into bouts of less than or greater than one minute is not an arbitrary one since energy for short-term endurance comes from the **anaerobic** systems in the working muscles, whereas energy for long-term endurance comes from the **aerobic** cycles. Clearly rugby is concerned with both types of endurance.

It is therefore valuable for the coach to consider in a little more depth, the general nature of the energy cycles before considering what is trainable and what should be trained.

## Energy cycles

Human beings obtain the energy they require to carry out the various tasks in life indirectly from the sun via the food they eat. The plants that they eat – for example, flour, potatoes, rice and fruit – are simply the stored energy of the sun. They also obtain energy by feeding on animals or the products of animals which, in their turn, have fed on plants – for example, meat, eggs or milk.

The human digestive system synthesizes these complex foods into more simple sugars and more simple fats. Energy is obtained either anaerobically from glucose, or as it is stored as glycogen, or aerobically from the fats depending on the intensity of work. Irrespective of the way energy is obtained, the proportion of the energy that is usable is the substance A.T.P. (adenosine triphosphate). This substance is the final molecule for the transmission of energy from whatever source and is thus seen as the basic unit of energy metabolism. There is always A.T.P. present in muscle cells but enough only for a very short period of intense work – for example, about one second of full-power sprinting.

We are going to look in greater detail at the nature of short-term, or anaerobic, endurance and at how to evaluate and train this mechanism.

## Short-term or anaerobic endurance

Anaerobic exercise means 'without air' or, more specifically, without oxygen. There

35

are three sets of circumstances under which this event takes place.

Firstly, at the very beginning of exercise, in the first 30 seconds or so, muscular work takes place without oxygen. An example is at the very ferocious start of an important game. A small **oxygen deficit** is built up which is repaid within a few minutes. During the period in which it is being repaid, the player finds it difficult to work at the level he would wish. When this deficit is repaid a **steady state** is reached and exercise seems easier. Older players often refer to this as a 'second wind'.

A second set of circumstances in which exercise takes place anaerobically, is when activity is of a very short duration and is completed in a second or so. An example would be a jump in the line-out or a snap shove in the scrum. In these cases, the body has insufficient time to get the oxygen transport systems working.

The final example of anaerobic exercise is when exercise is short but very intense. In this case it would last between 10 seconds and two minutes. This might be a play phase in a good quality game. This raises the possibility that rugby at the lower levels may be an aerobic activity and at the very top levels an anaerobic one.

It is clear then that there are different patterns of anaerobic exercise but it is important to remember that it is usual for the muscles to bring into play the anaerobic cycles to supplement the aerobic mechanisms when they are working near maximum.

The energy to do anaerobic work can come from two sources: from the **phosphagen system**, i.e. no lactic acid is produced; or from the **lactic acid system**.

## Phosphagen energy system

This is an energy store that operates without chemical penalties of any kind. It is distinct from glycolysis, the other source of anaerobic energy. With exercise the chemical phosphocreatine can be doubled or trebled in amount and can be depleted to about 10 per cent of resting levels. Even in its largest amount it can only be used to propel a rugby player sprinting at top speed for about 60m. At lower work rates, i.e. a lower level of anaerobic activity, there may be sufficient phosphocreatine for up to 20 or so seconds. Thus rugby players in some positions may well be using phosphocreatine for their brief moments of very intense activity.

## Lactic energy system

The main anaerobic energy system is called glycolysis (frequently referred to as anaerobic glycolysis). This system is concerned with the processing of the glucose from the blood or from the glycogen within the muscle cell, into the substance pyruvate and the release of energy. Although this system is less efficient, since considerably less energy is gained per glucose molecule than is obtained in the full aerobic process, there are a great number of enzymes that cause glycolysis. The net effect is that the cell can probably generate more energy anaerobically.

However, it is important that the pyruvate is cleared away rapidly since failure to do so results in the breakdown of this cycle. The pyruvate is converted into lactic acid in order to clear it away. This permits glycolysis to proceed for something in the order of 30 to 40 seconds at full power before the lactic acid produced brings the muscle cell to a virtual halt.

Over the space of a few minutes of work done at high intensity, 60gm of lactic acid can be produced (about 2oz). This amount can be diffused through the body fluids to give a blood concentration of about 125mg/100ml (about 12mM). Such a level may be regarded as a high one and would give the player a feeling of fatigue after only three to four minutes of intense activity. It is worth recording that lactic acid is removed from the bloodstream at about 100g per hour.

Given its importance in understanding training it is worth examining more closely the whole process of the production and removal of lactic acid. It is important to remember that there are considered to be three main types of muscle cells: the slow twitch (Type 1) fibres which work mainly aerobically; the Type 2A, or fast twitch, oxidative fibres which appear to work fairly equally aerobically or anaerobically; and the Type 2B, fast twitch, glycolytic fibres which work mainly anaerobically. Human muscles are composed of various mixtures and compositions of such cells. The ratio of muscle fibres in your body may well determine the position you occupy in the team. Those players who excel at sprinting or line-out leaping tend to have higher percentages of the two types of faster twitch fibres, whereas those players who appear to be in perpetual motion have equally high percentages of the slow twitch fibres.

No matter which mixture of fibres a player possesses the muscles always tend to recruit the three fibre types in the same order. The first to be used when working at the lower loads are the slow fibres and, as the work increases in severity, the type 2A fast fibres are activated. Should the load increase even further the anaerobic type 2B fast twitch fibres are recruited.

Players who are high in fast muscle fibres produce lactic acid very readily, while those who are low in these fibres do not. Thus the coach may need to direct the training of players who are high in fast twitch fibres towards aerobic endurance and, conversely, those high in slow twitch fibres towards anaerobic power.

Some lactic acid is recycled in its own cell. The fibres producing lactic acid shunt some of the chemical back across to pyruvate and then some will go on down into a process known as Krebs cycle for which pyruvate is a primary starting point. While some lactic acid may be taken up by neighbouring muscle fibres, especially those not so heavily engaged in highly demanding exercise such as Type 1 fibres, most of the lactic acid diffuses out of the cell, while the rest reaches the blood. Once in the blood much of it is neutralized by buffer chemicals, some of which create extra carbon dioxide which is exhaled. Finally the lactic acid is cleared from the blood by organs such as the kidneys, liver and, in some cases, the heart muscle which can utilize it as a fuel for the mitochondria by converting it to pyruvate. In the liver and kidneys, the lactic acid is built back up to glucose using a process called the 'coricycle'.

## Assessing anaerobic capacity

An important feature of successful physical preparation is the ability to measure a player prior to commencing a period of physical conditioning and thus being able to design a programme suited to your specific needs. Re-testing, following the training period, is important in helping to evaluate the success of that particular course of training.

Ideally, such testing is conducted in the laboratory, but where this is not possible (as in most cases) 'field tests' may be conducted at the club or sports centre. A good number of these 'field tests' are now available, many of which correlate highly with their more sophisticated laboratory-based counterparts. While these tests are often calibrated to help the programme designer to take into account differences in age and to compare performance against norms, perhaps their best use is in examining the player's progress.

**Laboratory measurement of anaerobic fitness**

It is difficult to test the phosphagen system, but muscle biopsy can be used to measure A.T.P. and phosphocreatine. The new measure of Nuclear Magnetic Resonance Spectroscopy (NMR) offers some potential as a non-invasive means of examining in detail selected aspects of the biochemistry of the muscles. This is achieved by recognizing substances by the wavelengths they emit when bombarded by strong electromagnetic fields.

Aside from these measures the most frequently encountered method of gaining some knowledge of the magnitude of the phosphagen energy component in a player is to select an appropriate activity and work him hard at that activity and record the 'recovery oxygen' or the so-called 'oxygen debt'. The recovery oxygen has three phases, of which only the first two are of any interest to the rugby player unless he is concerned with weight loss. The first, or fast phase, usually lasts about two minutes, and the second, or slow phase, is of 20 to 30 minutes duration.

The fast phase is thought to be the oxygen that is called upon to resynthesize the phosphocreatine. The greater the oxygen used by the player in the first two minutes of exercise, the greater the phosphagen system is considered to be.

It is also possible to test the lactic energy system by testing blood samples taken from the fingertip or ear lobe for lactic acid. Samples are taken at relevant periods throughout an increasing workload. A correlation between lactic acid and workload is recorded by plotting lactic acid levels every 2, 3 or 4 minutes as appropriate against workload.

The use of a progressive test is usually to find the 'anaerobic threshold' which is used to estimate what percentage of aerobic capacity the player can use. Measuring lactic acid gives a good indication of the blood level at sample time but what the recorded figure does not indicate is the rate of production and removal of the lactic acid. This production and removal of lactic acid, or its 'turnover' rate, may be a key feature in anaerobic fitness. Thus two performers may have the same blood level of lactic acid, say 12mM, but one player can 'turn over' the lactic acid five to ten times faster than the other.

It is worth stressing that the best possible purpose of testing is to enable the player to compare his performance with previous levels of performance. It is dangerous to use such tests for selection or for other purposes.

**Field tests of anaerobic fitness**

There is no field test of anaerobic muscle endurance that is simple to administer and suitable for all sports as there is for cardio-respiratory endurance (the step test). Each sport tends to design its own game-related tests. They usually take the form of a variety of activities such as dips, burpees, star-jumps etc. recorded as the number of repetitions completed in 30 or 60 seconds. If the selected exercises are game-related, and experience tells the coach that the muscle groups used simulate rugby activ-

ity, they are likely to be a useful indication of anaerobic fitness.

For example, the maximum number of repetitions correctly completed in 60 seconds with five minutes rest between exercise bouts for the following exercises would give a very good, and easy to administer, indication of this component of a player's fitness.

## Training for anaerobic endurance

It will be clear by now that by manipulating the work intensity, the duration of work and the periods of rest, the coach can develop both the phosphagen energy and lactic energy systems.

*Above: Training with a partner stimulates competition and makes training more varied and interesting. Also, you can help each other by recording one another's test results.*

### Phosphagen energy system – interval training

This system is of particular importance to players who are required to indulge in brief periods of very intensive work. Their in-training work periods therefore should last for not less than five nor more than 20 seconds. In total a target volume of six to eight minutes work is to be recommended. The emphasis in this form of training should always be on quality. Thus work should be near maximal, and adequate rest should be taken. A ratio, between repetitions, of work to rest of something in the region of 5:1 or 6:1 is acceptable with 5-10 minutes rest between each set. It is worth noting that some light activity during rest periods is preferable to passivity.

The manipulation of the work-rest ratio is often referred to as interval training. An example of this form of training using straight sprints or shuttle runs specifically to develop this energy system might be:

| Distance | Reps | Sets | Running time allowed | Recovery |
|----------|------|------|----------------------|----------|
| 50 metres | 6 | 3 | 7 secs | 45 secs walk between reps. 5 mins. jog between sets. |

### Lactic energy system

As a general rule, this system begins to be taxed at about 80 per cent of maximum effort for a set duration of exercise. Thus exercise should be performed at no less than 90 per cent maximum effort in order to ensure the maximum recruitment of most muscle fibres.

A work time of 40-60 secs is the norm with occasional bouts of work up to two minutes. Any longer than two minutes and the load on anaerobic lactic acid will not be increased and the aerobic energy supply will be recruited. A set volume of about two minutes is therefore maximum with about one minute the more usual.

A total target volume of somewhere between 10 and 20 minutes is recommended. The work:rest ratio between repetitions for training this system is 1:2 with approximately 10 minutes of active rest (jogging, for example) between each set. The work:rest ratio should change gradually to 1:1 and then 2:1 as the player works through the schedule. For example, in shuttle running the player would start by running for 30 secs with 60 secs active rest, would go through 30 secs rest, and move to 60 secs work with 30 secs rest.

Running, skipping, shuttle runs, step-ups and short sprinting are all suitable forms of exercise.

An example of the type of training appropriate for training this energy system is shown in the table.

| Distance/mode | Reps | Sets | Time/Intensity Allowed | Recovery |
|---------------|------|------|------------------------|----------|
| 200m | 6 | 2 | 35 secs. | Jog 2 mins. between reps. Jog 10 mins. between sets |
| Skipping | 10 x 30 secs. | 1 | 180 skips min. | 2 mins. jog between reps. |
| Step-ups | 5 x 1 | 2 | 60 steps min. | 2 mins. jog between reps. 10 mins. jog between sets |

# CHAPTER FOUR

# DEVELOPING STRENGTH

Although the best rugby players are not always the strongest players, strength is a very important feature in good performance in almost all positions on the rugby field. Indeed, in some positions, such as prop, strength is of paramount importance.

In addition, it is important to note that strength is a key feature of several other aspects of performance. For example, it is a major factor in *power* since:

power = force x velocity

While it is clear that the major need for most playing positions is power, an increase in strength results in the potential to apply more force and consequently to generate more power.

The contribution that strength makes to endurance is exemplified by the fact that if a person moves a resistance through a particular range of motion for 100 repetitions and later increases his strength by 50 per cent he would be able to move the same resistance with considerably less discomfort.

An equally important factor when considering strength is its value in protecting players from injury in such a high speed collision sport as rugby. This is achieved by increasing joint stability.

## What is strength?

Strength is the ability of the body or its segments to apply force. However, many people in rugby view strength as simply the contractile force of muscles, but it is more complex than that since there are three factors that interact in the production of strength:

1 The combined contractile forces of those muscles (agonists) that cause the movement.
2 The ability to integrate the agonistic muscles with the antagonistic and the neutralizer and stabilizer muscles involved in the activity.
3 The mechanical ratios of the lever (bone) arrangements involved in the movement.

There are two basic types of strength: static strength (isometric); and dynamic strength (isotonic). Dynamic strength can be classified further into a concentric phase, where the muscle shortens, and an eccentric phase when the muscle goes back to its original length. Both these phases need to be trained in a proper schedule.

Although static and dynamic strength are related to a degree, they are not synonymous and it is possible to develop either form of strength without developing the other kind to the same extent. While it is much easier and more accurate to record static strength, it is in fact dynamic strength that is utilized far more frequently in rugby performance.

It is important to point out, from the outset, that there is no perfect strength training method. Each of a number of methods has its advantages and disadvantages since players vary in their responsiveness to the particular form of training selected. Thus the selection of the form of strength training to be used cannot be an exact science. It should, therefore, be determined by the variables of purpose, available equipment, enjoyment and personal preference. Experience has shown that the majority of players find weight training to be the most satisfying training method since they are able to see progress.

## Phasing of the programme

When planning a fitness training programme, the requirements for the various phases of the year differ. The programme can be divided into:

1 The closed or non-playing phase
2 The pre-season phase
3 The start of the season phase
4 The full competitive season

Players should train on strength-related activities three times a week in the first three phases and once or, if possible, twice in the last phase.

### 1 The closed or non-playing phase

This phase is the best time to introduce strength training. It allows you to follow a comprehensive schedule which will provide a basis of general conditioning, mobility and strength. This period should last about 4-6 weeks and should be directed towards an increase in strength and endurance.

### 2 The pre-season phase

Some 4-8 weeks prior to the season the number of exercises are decreased and those exercises of a massive nature will be included. Repetitions are decreased and resistance is increased. Training at this stage becomes more specific and focuses on your specific role.

### 3 The start-of-season phase

About one month prior to the season commencing, you should use a schedule directed at power building.

### 4 The full competitive phase

Once the season is in full swing, the objective of this part of the training programme is to maintain the basis of power which has been created.

## Important considerations

### 1 Safety factors

Before embarking on details of specific weight-training activities it is important to note a number of critical safety factors. While it is true to say that there is the usual quota of sprains, strains and tears which are associated with any form of vigorous exercise, strength training is relatively free from temporary or chronic injury problems if the following safety precautions are observed:

1 Avoid training alone if possible.
2 Keep weights close to the body when lifting.
3 Use the correct technique in all exercises.
4 Always lift from the floor with a flat back and bent knees.
5 Never stretch cold muscles.
6 Because of the damage to growing tissue, no serious weight-training programme should be commenced until it appears that the young player has ceased to grow. This is usually somewhere in the 17-19 years age range. Prior to stopping growing, young players should be coached in correct weight-training technique, with an emphasis on light weights with high repetitions, rather than on heavy weights.

### 2 Points to consider

When planning a strength-training programme, you should take the following into consideration:

● Resistance should be carried through the full range of the motion of the joint and should be directly opposed to the direction of the body movement.

● To ensure maximum results some body parts need to be isolated. This is done because weaker muscles should not be used to transmit the resistance when the trainer wishes to apply maximal force.

● Normally strength will develop more quickly in those muscles that are well short of their potential strength. The rate of strength acquisition decreases as the muscle approaches its full potential, known as 'end strength'.

● While the mechanical advantage of a muscle is less than maximal when the muscle is fully extended, its contractile force is maximal in that position. Thus as the muscles go through their range of contraction, the mechanical ratio changes resulting in a strength curve. It would be logical, when planning, to include a variable resistance to match the strength curve.

● The fundamental concepts of overload and progressive resistance must be applied in a strength-training programme. These principles apply regardless of the particular method of training used.

● Since significant strength gains result only in the exercised muscles, exercises must be selected to work the particular muscles in which strength is to be developed.

● Three sessions per week (i.e. at least every second day such as Monday, Wednesday and Friday) against heavy resistance have been found to be most beneficial in strength training.

● Use near-maximal weight for few repetitions, e.g. four sets of 4-6 repetitions (70-80% maximum) on each particular muscle group.

## Developing strength

As in all forms of training the coach/trainer should overload the player. That is to say,

muscles must be contracted against heavy resistance and the resistance must be increased as the muscles develop strength. Under these broad principles, a number of approaches to developing strength exist. Bearing in mind that any form of exercise that applies heavier than usual resistance stimulates an increase in strength, the following common forms of strength building are encountered.

**Exercises using body weight**
If sophisticated apparatus is not readily available to the player it is still possible to plan some very worthwhile strength-training programmes by simply using the body weight of the player. These exercises are especially suitable for the player under about 19 years of age since it is advisable to restrict the use of heavy weights until after puberty. Additionally, weights may be fixed to the body as progress is made. A programme based on such exercise as: press-ups, sit-ups, rope climbs, chins on beam or bar, single leg squats and dips on a chair or between parallel bars, will be beneficial.

Using these exercises it is possible to maintain progress by manipulating the following variables:
● Lengthening the levers.
● Increasing the number of repetitions.
● Amending the starting position.
● Performing the repetitions more quickly.
● Tying some form of weight to the waist (as in chins or dips) or placing a weight behind the neck (as in sit-ups).

**Exercises using heavy resistance**
Some exercises involve heavy resistance against external movable resistance such as multi-gym equipment or equipment using 'free' weights. Since resistance can

*continued on page 45*

43

## Single leg squat

This exercise uses the player's own body weight, and is thus especially suitable for players who are under 19 years of age.

**1** Stand up straight with feet close together and place your hands to the sides at the back of your head. Raise one leg, bending the knee, to balance on the other leg.

**2** Now squat down on your single supporting leg, keeping the other leg bent without touching the ground with your back foot. Hold for a few seconds and return to the original standing position. Repeat the exercise with the other leg. Do 6-8 repetitions with each leg .

be increased progressively, this method provides perhaps the greatest potential for increasing strength.

On page 54 there is an example of a strength schedule which shifts to power and utilizes exercises using heavy resistance. This is, however, a schedule specific to a back row forward. The novice may wish to commence with a programme suitable for basic strength training for all players. Illustrated below is an example of such a programme.

Remember that it is very important to exercise both the **concentric** phase (where the muscle shortens), and the **eccentric** phase (where the muscle goes back to its original length). Remember also to work through the full range of the movement.

Complete 6-8 repetitions on each exercise in 3 sets before moving on to the next exercise. Complete the exercises in the order indicated. Work around 70-80 per cent maximum possible for one repetition. Adequate recovery between sets and exercises is permitted. Remember to warm up and cool down.

## Leg press

**1** Sit tall in the seat with the hips and back solidly against the seat, and your knees at an angle of approximately 90 degrees.
**2** Keeping your head and chest up, grasp the grips at the sides of the chair.
**3** Press forcefully to extend the legs fully. Return to the starting position slowly and under control.

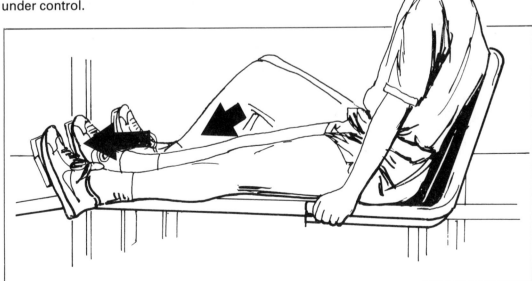

## Leg extension *below*

**1** Lock your ankles at right angles under the rollers.

**2** Lift slowly, concentrating on making a smooth, driving lift. Don't kick.

**3** Lock out your legs at the top of the lift and then lower under control. You should stay sitting upright throughout with your back against the rest, grasping the rails with both hands.

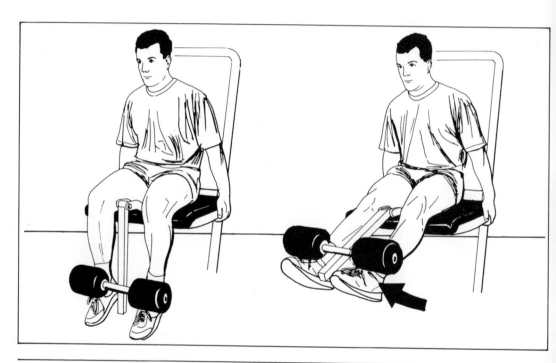

## Leg curls *right*

**1** Lie face down and place your heels under the roller. Line up your knee joints with the hinge or pivot pin.

**2** Holding the frame, pull up the heels as far as possible. Return to the starting position.

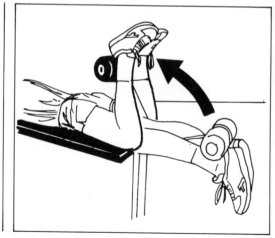

## Calf raises

**1** Stand with toes on a raised object, with the bar comfortably on the shoulders.

**2** Drive up onto your toes, raising your heels off the ground, to full extension. Lower the heels to the floor under control.

## Leg abductions

**1** Attach cable and pully to your left ankle.
**2** Supporting your body with your right arm and keeping your spine at right angles to the floor, concentrate on making long steady sweeps with your left leg. Repeat with your right leg.

## Chest exercise

**1** Position the seat so that the upper arms are parallel to the floor. Grasp the pads with your hands.

**2** Keeping your back and head against the seat, use a smooth, hard drive to bring your elbows together. Close the pads under control and open again.

## Long cable pulls

**1** Smoothly pull the cable out up to your chest.

**2** Smoothly and slowly return the cable to the starting position.

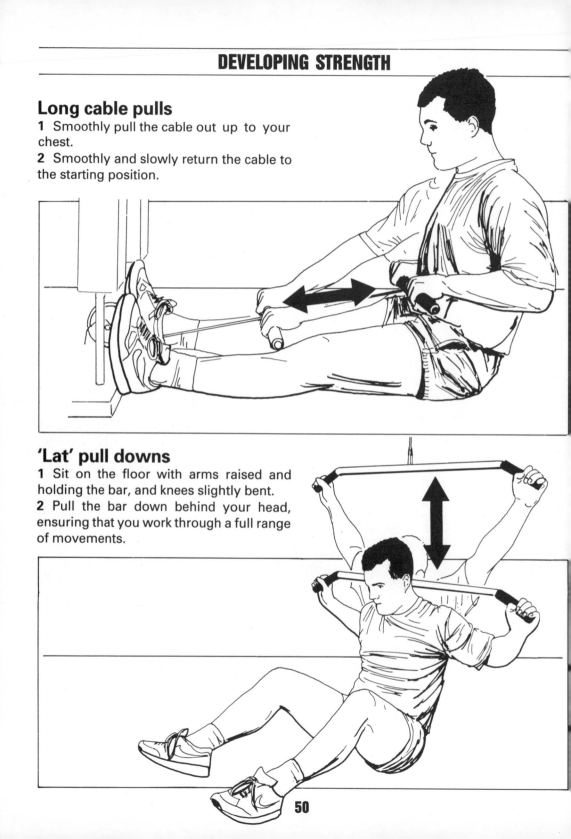

## 'Lat' pull downs

**1** Sit on the floor with arms raised and holding the bar, and knees slightly bent.

**2** Pull the bar down behind your head, ensuring that you work through a full range of movements.

## Bent arm pull overs

**1** Lie back on the bench, resting the bar on the lower chest with a normal grip and the elbows at the sides.

**2** Raise the bar off the chest and backwards overhead until it gets to the bottom of the range of movements.

## Arm curls

**1** Stand with feet apart, holding the bar in both hands.
**2** Slowly raise the bar to shoulder height. Lower again under control.

**Repeated hard physical work**

Vigorous and repeated hard physical work or athletic performance will increase strength but, since this often lacks the potential to increase resistance progressively, it is a less efficient method of improvement.

**Exercises involving isokinetic contraction**

One modification of isotonic exercise is the development of isokinetic exercises involving the use of a machine which controls the speed of the movement. The machine prevents the dissipation of muscular energy in acceleration and provides resistance which is proportional to the input of the muscular force and the alterations in skeletal levers throughout the range of motion. To put it more simply, it compensates for those differences in the muscle force which can be developed at various angles of a joint and is thus able to provide maximal variable resistance at any angle. These variable resistance machines are a somewhat recent phenomenon which may develop in popularity.

**Exercises involving isometric contraction**

The use of muscle tension, known as isometric contraction, which is applied against another body part or a fixed object has also been shown to develop the body in terms of strength and appearance. Using this method, unlike the previous three in which the muscle shortens (isotonic), means that the muscle does not change in length and the body segments do not move.

Once the coach has ensured the successful completion of an all-round strengthening programme, he should analyse the specific activities for which he wishes his player to increase his strength. He thus determines the contributing movements and can then select the exercises that work the muscles that cause these movements and build them into the programme.

**Resistance running**

This form of exercise is simply where running is made more difficult for the player in order to develop strength (it can also be used to develop endurance or indeed both of these qualities). There are a number of forms of resistance running that can help the player to develop his strength. These include:

- Repetition uphill sprints.
- Cross-country running.
- Running through sandhills or snow.
- Running wearing a weighted belt.
- Sprinting pulling some object (e.g. tractor tyre, garden roller or sledge).

- Sprinting against resistance (e.g. harness held by another player).

As a general rule, resistance running should be used perhaps once a week. It is also useful to build in some variety, and to ensure that backs in particular do not shorten their stride length. In contrast it may be useful for forwards to emphasize short strides to develop the drive needed in the ruck and scrum and in breaking the tackle.

*Below: Resistance running. The player tries to run forward while two other players attempt to hold him back. This exercise is useful for developing strength and can be used effectively by both backs and forwards.*

## Sample schedule

Listed below is an example of a strength/power training plan for a rugby player (back row forward or group B).

### Closed season

**Aim:** Learning fitness and mobility. Use short rests. Keep pulse rate high.

| Exercise | Sets/Reps |
|---|---|
| Abdominals | 3 x 10-30 reps |
| 2-hand curl | 3 x 10-20 reps |
| Back squats | 3 x 10-20 reps |
| Press behind neck | 3 x 10-20 reps |
| Bent forward rowing | 3 x 10-20 reps |
| Bench press | 3 x 10-20 reps |
| Power cleans | 3 x 10-20 reps |
| High pull-up | 3 x 10-20 reps |

### Start of season

**Aim:** Power build-up.

| Exercise | Sets/Reps |
|---|---|
| Power cleans | Pyramid |
| | 5 x 4 x 3 x 2 x 1 |
| Heave press | 5 x 4 x 3 x 2 x 1 |
| Squat jumps | 3 x 5 reps |
| Dead lifts | 3 x 5 reps |

**Note:** Plyometric exercises can be included here.

### Pre-season

**Aim:** Strength build-up.

| Exercise | Sets/Reps |
|---|---|
| Power cleans | 5 x 6 reps |
| Back squats | 5 x 6 reps |
| Lunges | 5 x 5 reps |
| Heave press | 5 x 5 reps |
| Bench press | 5 x 5 reps |

### Throughout season

**Aim:** Power maintenance.

| Exercise | Sets/Reps |
|---|---|
| Power cleans | 5 x 4 reps |
| Heave press | 5 x 4 reps |
| Squat jumps | 5 x 4 reps |
| High pulls | 5 x 4 reps |

## Abdominals

Perform as you would for a normal sit-up with a weight behind the neck. Wrap it in a towel to make it more comfortable.

## Two-hand curls

1 Hold the bar, shoulder width, across the front of the thighs.
2 Bend the arms strongly at the elbows until the bar rests on the chest, making sure that the bar is kept close to the body. Lower the bar under control.

## Back squats

1 Stand with your feet comfortably apart at normal hip width with the bar resting across the upper back.
2 Bend the knees and squat down. Gently rebound at the lower position (less than 90 degrees) and rise up strongly by straightening the legs.

## Press behind neck

1 With your feet astride, rest the bar comfortably behind the neck.
2 Press the barbell straight up to full arms length. Lower under control.

## Bent forward rowing

1 Keeping your back flat and head up with arms straight and knuckles to the front, make sure that your hands and feet are quite wide apart.
2 Bend your knees slightly and pull the bar strongly up to the chest by bending the arms and raising the elbows sideways. Then lower the barbell carefully under control.

## Bench press

1 Lie on your back on a bench with the bar resting on your chest, keeping your forearms vertical and below the bench and

your arms wider than shoulder width.

2 From this position, press the barbell up vigorously to arm's length, and then lower it again under control.

## Power clean

1 Stand with your feet shoulder width apart under the bar, and grasp the bar with your knuckles forward and back flat.

2 Extend your legs and back vigorously, only using the arms when the bar passes mid-thigh level.

3 Dip to catch the barbell and stand up. Lower the bar to the thighs and, bending the knees, lower the bar to the start position.

## High pulls

1 With arms wide and knuckles forward, hold the bar across the front of the shins. Keep your back straight, your eyes looking forwards and your chin up.

2 Pull the bar up to chin level with the chest held high and the hips slightly forwards as the body rises up high on to the toes.

## Heave press

1 Pull the barbell up from the floor to the chest, dipping the knees to get to the starting position.

2 From this position, extend the legs and arms vigorously to stand up straight until the arms are fully extended.

## Lunges

1 Start with the bar held high across the chest. Step one leg forward while the rear foot should point straight ahead with the heel raised off the floor.

2 Lower the body and the weight by bending both legs. Make sure that the forward knee is in front of the forward foot.

# Recent innovations in strength/power training

## Plyometric methods

There is some evidence that mechanical efficiency is greatest when flexion of a muscle is immediately followed by its extension. This so-called *elastic rebound* has been developed into the method of training known as **plyometrics**.

The development of plyometric training has appeared to be of potential value in increasing leg power, e.g. in line-outs (depth jumping) and increasing acceleration (plyometric circuits).

Essentially plyometric exercises are the link between strength and speed. They are the opposite of weight training which operates on a concentric-eccentric sequence. Plyometrics therefore operate in an eccentric-concentric fashion. Thus a degree of eccentric work is normally achieved prior to the concentric work occurring. This eccentric phase involves varying degrees of muscle lengthening sometimes referred to as pre-load or pre-stretch.

Plyometrics are used to develop jumping ability, acceleration and speed off the mark. The training can take many forms. For example:

1 **Standing jumps:** e.g. standing long jump, triple jump, standing five hops

2 **Short-approach jumps**: e.g. 30m hop on left leg, rest, then another 30m hop on left leg (aiming to do the minimum number of hops possible over the chosen distance).

3 **Sequential bounding**: e.g. hop/step/hop/ step; hop hop/step step/ hop hop etc. Try to aim for a regular rhythm.

4 **Endurance bounding**: e.g. 20m giant strides (steps), 20m hop on left leg, 20m

giant strides etc. Perform sets of 3 reps. with a five-minute recovery period. Time each set with a stop-watch and record the times achieved.

**5 Depth jumping:** (from box or benches): e.g. from height (both legs), for distance (both legs), for height and distance (single leg).

Plyometric exercises can be of great motivational value provided that they are correctly done and regularly recorded. The first three outlined here are more suitable for beginners, while the other two are for post-pubescent, well-conditioned sports-people only. It is unwise to take part in plyometric sessions if you have any history of lower limb injury. In the interests of safety, the following precautions should be observed when performing bounding exercises:

## Precautions for bounding exercises

● Surfaces should be dry, non-slip and resilient (e.g. mats on gym floor, springy turf etc.).
● Footwear should be sufficiently padded to reduce shock, particularly in the heel region.
● Foot placement and landing contacts should be in the line of bounding – in other words, don't land with your toes pointing to the side!
● The trunk should be upright; land on the flat of the foot (not the heel or toe) with a dynamic impact. The foot should be in front of the hip, not out to the side or directly underneath.
● Push upwards to drive into the next action.
● Place the accent on quality: do the exercises when you are still fresh. Stop when the quality of performance starts to decline.
● Over-indulgence in plyometric exercises can cause considerable stiffness. Don't overdo them.
● The potential of plyometrics is limited only by the imagination of the coach.
● There may be some benefit in using slightly lower boxes for heavier players, especially early in the training programme.

## Sample plyometrics

Listed below are a number of sample plyometric exercises that are of value to all groups of players.

**1 Hopping for height and distance:** single leg hops conducted consecutively. 1 set of 10/12 repetitions.

**2 Knee driving:** 1 set of 10 reps. each leg.

**3 Crouch bounds:** 1 set of 10. Stand in a crouched squat position and leap forwards to obtain as great a distance as possible.

**4 Depth jumping:**
(1) Stand on stable box. Jump up from the box, land and then jump for distance.
(2) As above but make a sequence from one box to the floor to a second box.
(3) Jump from box, land and accelerate for 5-10 metres.
(4) Stand on box. Jump down to the right onto right foot only. Jump back on to box and then to the left on the left foot.

# CHAPTER FIVE

# DIET AND NUTRITION

Diet and nutrition play an essential role in getting fit for rugby. Since improvements in levels of fitness are brought about by the body adapting to the demands of training, good nutrition is of great value in facilitating that adaptation and in helping you achieve high levels of performance. It also enables you to recover between essential training sessions and the matches themselves.

You should ensure that your food intake matches the demands placed upon your body during training and in carrying out your daily routine. Remember it is important that you consume sufficient energy in the form of carbohydrates to maintain the stored energy within the muscle. Low intakes of carbohydrates result in low glycogen stores.

If you are a serious player, you need not restrict your meals to traditional mealtimes since this can lead to gorging. Fit in eating to suit your training and playing requirements. Smaller and more frequent meals help, and snacks in the mid-morning or afternoon can be useful on days when you have an evening training session or match. It is also important to rest and give the body time to recover. On such days be sure to refuel carbohydrate stores.

It is a common mistake to select simple carbohydrates such as confectionery and sweet foods to provide the carbohydrates in your diet. Instead you should select complex carbohydrates carefully and remember that, contrary to popular myth, there is no great need to eat vast amounts of red meat. Indeed, red meats are high in fat (e.g. duck, pork, lamb and beef) and it is better to replace them with lean or white meats such as chicken or turkey or with vegetable proteins. It is also sensible to replace oily fish such as tuna or mackerel with white fish, e.g. cod, haddock or plaice.

A further useful guide to sensible eating is to replace your consumption of fried foods with foods that are grilled, steamed or quickly stir-fried, and avoid the addition of fat in such forms as gravy and sauces, or butter on jacket potatoes.

Additionally a high fluid intake of fresh water or fresh fruit juice (rich in electrolytes) helps to avoid dehydration pre- and post-training.

## Body composition

Many players, especially forwards, regard body weight as an important factor in performance. However, it is lean body mass that is the important factor since body fat is of little value to a rugby player. Indeed, around 15 or more per cent body fat can actually be a limitation to performance. As a general rule, the lower your body fat rating the better. When looking at non-athletic populations, the medical world suggests that for the adult male a body fat rating of 20 per cent is too high and a rating of 25 per cent or more takes a man into the 'obese' category. A single figure value is essential for the serious rugby player.

Even a quick glance at many rugby players, including those playing at a high level, shows that there is a good deal of work still to be done in re-educating and encouraging players to change their body composition and to replace fat with muscle mass.

## Assessment of body composition

A useful starting point is to assess each player's body composition by using skin-fold calipers which measure the thickness of flesh at a number of sites on the body. Measurements recorded on the front and back of upper arms, beneath the shoulder blade and just above the hip can be aggregated and, using a simple chart, can be transformed into a percentaged body fat with a reasonable degree of accuracy. This often serves to interest and motivate players.

## Reducing body fat

The best way to reduce body fat is to take regular aerobic activity. While you should examine your diet closely and generally reduce your calorific intake (especially alcohol!), you also need to avoid 'crash' diets and aim instead for a gradual shift in the fat/lean body mass relationship over months rather than days. Ideally, weight reduction should simply be an adjustment of eating habits to consume a more balanced and/or smaller amount of food. Crash diets are of doubtful benefit since the normal functions of the body need to be maintained. Indeed, during severe dieting, the loss of weight over the first few weeks is mainly the body's carbohydrate reserves and fluids rather than fat, and with low reserves of these, training will be both tiring and difficult. A weight loss of around 1kg/2lb a week is a useful target.

The old notion of players turning up for pre-season training 10 or so kilograms/22lb overweight is one that should be condemned to the folklore of yesteryear, and all players should be encouraged to take a careful interest in what and how much they eat.

Since most traditional programmes generally involve the drastic reduction of carbohydrate intake, you need to amend such recommendations to enable you to maintain the muscle glycogen levels that enable you to continue exercising.

The best compromise if you are intent on fat loss is to reduce energy intake while ensuring that nutrient density and carbohydrates are kept high. All foods should be low in energy and high in carbohydrates, trace elements, minerals and vitamins: in other words, a low-fat, high-carbohydrate diet. In effect, you should remove all visible fat from your food intake (such as lard, butter, oils, fat on meat), as well as the fat that is 'hidden' in such foods as chips, crisps, cakes, biscuits, cheese, red meat and oily fish. Such foods should be replaced by low-fat foods, and you should try to eat complex carbohydrates (such as wholemeal bread, pulses and legumes, potatoes, nuts, fresh fruit, dried fruit and wholemeal pasta). If you are already eating a reduced fat diet, you may need to adjust the overall quantity of food.

Combining these shifts in your eating habits with your regular training programme should result in fat loss. It is important to remember, however, that we are not so much concerned with the weight recorded by the weighing machine as the ratio of fat to lean body mass of that weight.

Once you have adopted these guidelines and have achieved the desired body composition, you should then understand how to maintain that ratio.

## Increasing muscle mass

It is an interesting comment on our society that very few players seek help and advice to gain weight in the form of lean body mass. It is easy to gain body fat but gains in muscle mass are achieved only as a result of intensive training. The notion that eating a very high protein diet will increase muscle mass is a false one since excess protein is either stored as fat or excreted from the body. Adopting such abnormal eating practices may create dangerous life-long habits which can increase the risk of heart disease as well as reduce your appetite for those important foods that are high in carbohydrates.

Perhaps the best approach to gaining muscle mass is to eat a high-carbohydrate diet which ensures that your glycogen stores are full prior to each fitness training session. By matching the increases in the volume and intensity of training to your diet, muscle mass should increase. The failure to refuel adequately between training sessions, is clearly demonstrated by an excessive and constant feeling of tiredness and, in some cases, the condition labelled ketosis, which is marked by the smell of peardrops on the breath. Both these conditions indicate that the body is lacking in carbohydrates.

In practice it is difficult to increase only muscle mass, and some gains in the fat stores do occur. However, these can be reduced once the desired level of muscle mass has been achieved.

## Foods high in carbohydrates

**Complex:**
**Cereals:** Weetabix, Shredded Wheat, Puffed Wheat, porridge, etc.
**Dried fruit:** currants, sultanas, apricots, prunes, etc.
**Fresh fruit:** apples, bananas, oranges, pears, grapes, etc.
**Nuts:** peanuts (unsalted), brazil nuts, chestnuts, almonds, etc.
**Canned fruit:** (no sugar): fruit in unsweetened natural juice.
**Pulses and legumes:** peas, lentils, beans (haricot, baked, kidney), pearl barley, etc.
**Wholemeal bread flour:** loaves and crispbreads.
**Wholemeal foods:** pastas, brown rice

**Simple:**
**Drinks:** drinking chocolate, malted bedtime drinks.
**Confectionery:** chocolate, toffee, fudge, etc.

**Sugar:** syrup, jam, marmalade, etc.
**Sugar coated foods:** breakfast cereals, cakes, biscuits.
**Desserts:** milky puddings, sweet custard, fruit yoghurt, jelly, cheesecake.
**Note:** You should increase the complex carbohydrate foods in your diet, and reduce the simple carbohydrates, many of which contain refined sugar and 'empty' calories and have little nutritional goodness.

## Sources of protein
**Animal protein:**
Fish, shellfish.
Eggs.
Meat, poultry, offal.
Milk, cheese, yoghurt.

**Vegetable protein:**
Beans: haricot, butter, baked etc.
Bread, potatoes, cereals, pasta, rice, etc.
Nuts and seeds.
Pulses, lentils, peas.

# CHAPTER SIX

# FLEXIBILITY

The concept of flexibility is an important one in rugby since it is both an aid to performance and can help in the prevention of injury. Flexibility is described best as the range of motion in a given joint or combination of joints. Three factors are involved in flexibility:

1 The bone and ligament structure of the joint.
2 The size and nature of the bulk surrounding the joint.
3 The extensibility of muscles whose tendons cross the joint.

Of these three factors the third one is of greatest concern to those players seeking to increase flexibility. In developing flexibility it is useful to bear in mind that there are three categories:

## Basic flexibility

This is the range of movement possible with external assistance using a partner, some form of equipment or some other similar method.

## Active flexibility

This is the range of movement possible by the joints themselves without external assistance. That is to say, the player's own relevant muscle group pulls across the joint stretching muscle ligament and connective tissue on the other side of the joint.

## Kinetic flexibility

This is the range of movement possible due to the momentum of joint actions, e.g. swinging the leg high.

All flexibility improvement sessions for rugby players should be constructed along the following lines:

1 The session should commence by raising body temperature by performing mixed activities such as jogging and general warm-up exercises in very warm, heavy clothing. It is preferable for this to take place in a warm environment.
2 Active flexibility work should follow for each joint action.
3 Move on to passive mobility using apparatus or partners.
4 Kinetic flexibility.
5 The session should peak with specific flexibility exercises combined with strength and technique.
6 Finish with a warm-down.

# An example of a flexibility session

Listed below are a number of useful examples of:
**1** Active stretching    **2** Passive stretching    **3** Kinetic stretching

These are valuable for all rugby players and are arranged in a suitable order for a flexibility training session.

## *1 Active stretching*

### Head rotations

**1** Stand erect with your hands on your thighs, and feet shoulder-width apart.
**2** Rotate your head slowly through a full circle from the point where your chin is on your chest to the head-back position. Then repeat the exercise in the opposite direction.

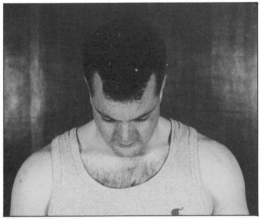
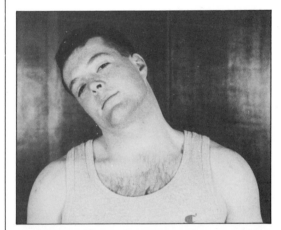
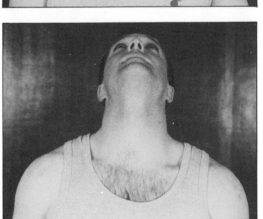
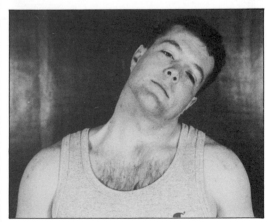

## Upper body stretch (1)

**1** Interlace your fingers with the palms facing upwards.

**2** Reach away as far as possible. This exercise stretches the trunk, shoulders and arms as well as, to a lesser degree, the legs.

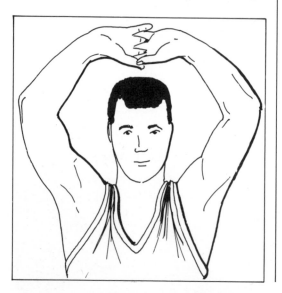

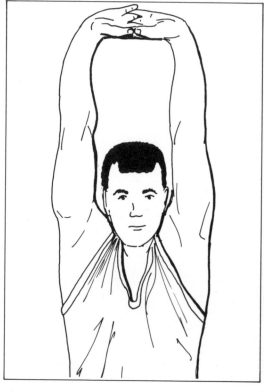

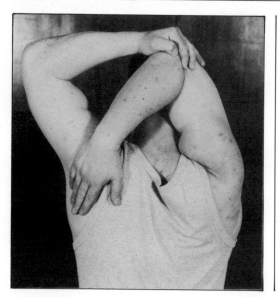

## Upper body stretch (2) *left*

**1** With the right hand, reach for the left shoulder blade.

**2** Stretch the fingers and, using the left hand to steady the right one, stretch. This stretches the lateral trunk, shoulder and arm muscles. Repeat with the other arm.

## Posterior thigh muscles (hamstring) stretch *opposite*

With feet comfortably apart and knees partially bent, bend forwards allowing your arms to hang loosely and stretch the hamstrings and buttocks.

## Front of thighs (quadriceps) stretch *below*

Stand with your feet comfortably apart, arms loosely at the sides and knees partially bent, stretching the large muscle groups at the front of the thighs.

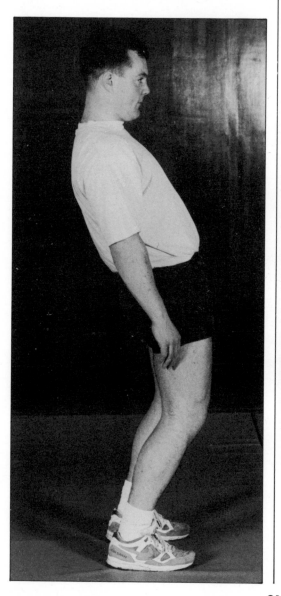

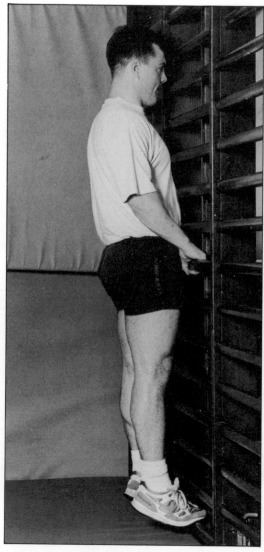

## Lower leg (calf muscles) stretch *above*

1 Stand with your toes on a raised object and hold on for support with your arms.
2 Lower your heels as far as possible towards the floor and then raise them. Repeat several times. Try to make sure that the heels at no point touch the floor.

## Upper trunk stretch *below*

Lie on your stomach, pushing your upper body back until your arms are fully extended. Keep your pelvis on the floor and your head back.

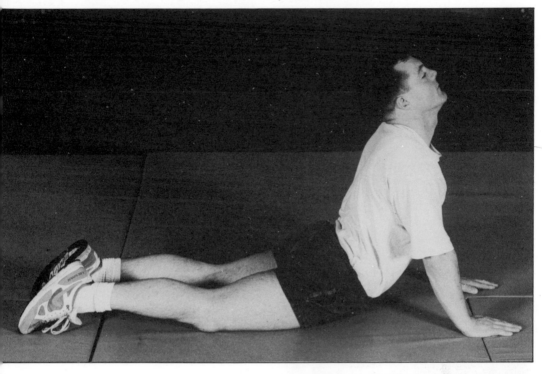

## Groin stretch *right*

Sitting with the ankles and knees pointing outwards, push down gently on the knees. Release and repeat.

## Lower back stretch

**1** Lie on your back and hold each leg just below the knees.

**2** Pull your knees up slowly towards the chest and hold.

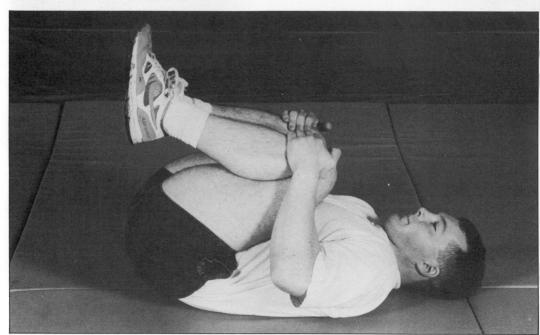

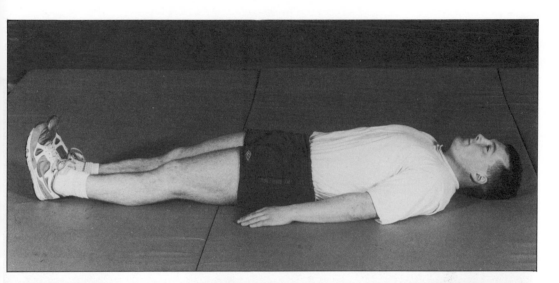

## Hip and upper back stretch

1  Start from a lying position on your back.
2  Holding your legs straight, pull them up and over your head until your toes touch the ground behind the head. This exercise strengthens the hip flexors and abdominal muscles as well as stretching the hamstrings and back.

## 2 Passive stretching

## Shoulder chest stretch (1)
Your partner applies pressure to bring the
hands together behind the back.

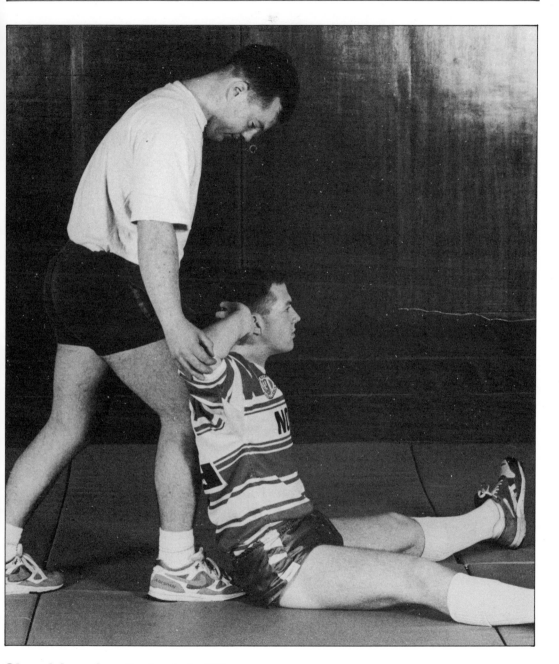

## Shoulder-chest stretch (2)

Sit with your legs spread, and your fingers locked behind the neck. Your partner places his knee in your back, and then he grasps your elbows and pulls your arms back.

## Upper back stretch *above*
**1** Assume the position shown.
**2** Your partner pushes downwards on your lower back.

## Lower back stretch *opposite*
**1** Sit on the floor with your legs spread.
**2** Your partner applies pressure forwards and downwards. Repeat to the front and to either side.

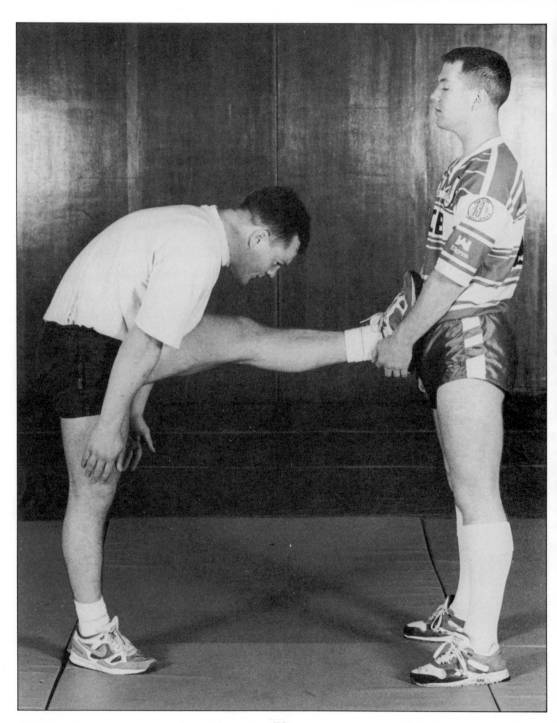

## Hamstrings stretch (1) *above*

**1** Player A does the splits with the front knee locked, toes pointing upwards. His weight supported by his arms and rear leg.

**2** Player B gently raises Player A's front leg off the floor.

## Hamstrings stretch (2) *opposite*

**1** Place one heel in your partner's hands. about waist height.

**2** Keeping the legs straight, try to touch your knee with your nose.

## Lower trunk-groin stretch *right*

**1** Assume the position as illustrated, grasping your partner's knees.

**2** Pull his legs and lower body towards you.

## Groin stretch

**1** Player A grasps Player B's lower leg and puts one hand on B's lower back.

**2** Player A then raises B's leg to shoulder level, keeping one hand on B's lower back for support.

## 3 Kinetic stretching

### High leg swing (for hips)

**1** Stand upright with the back straight, holding on to a wall bar with one hand. Extend one leg back behind you.

**2** Drive the leg forwards as high as possible, rising onto the toes of the supporting foot as you do so. Try to increase your range of swing.

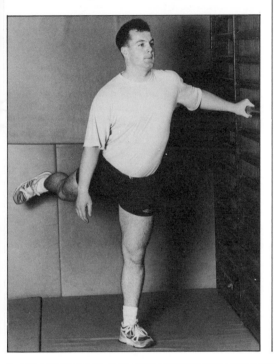

### Back raises (back) *right*

**1** Lean over backwards to hold on to the wall bars behind you.

**2** Keeping your feet flat on the ground, lift your abdomen as high as possible. Lower again under control.

## Trunk circles (abdominals)

**1** Stand with feet and arms shoulder width apart, and arms raised high.

**2** Bend over to one side, lowering your arms, and then sweep down and forwards in front of you so that your arms are nearly touching the floor.

**3** Move your arms upwards to the other side in a circular movement and then back to the starting position.

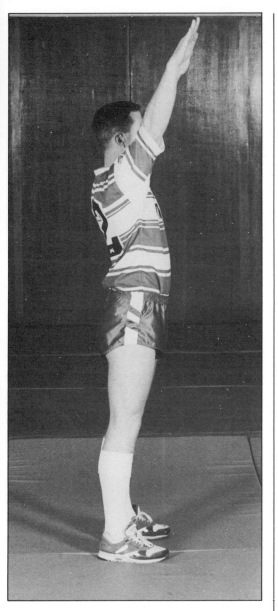

## Arm circling (shoulder girdle)

**1** Stand with feet flat on the ground and eyes looking forwards, arms by sides.
**2** Raise your arms in a circular movement up to shoulder height and then extend them above your head.
**3** Lower the arms continuing the circular movement backwards behind the shoulders.

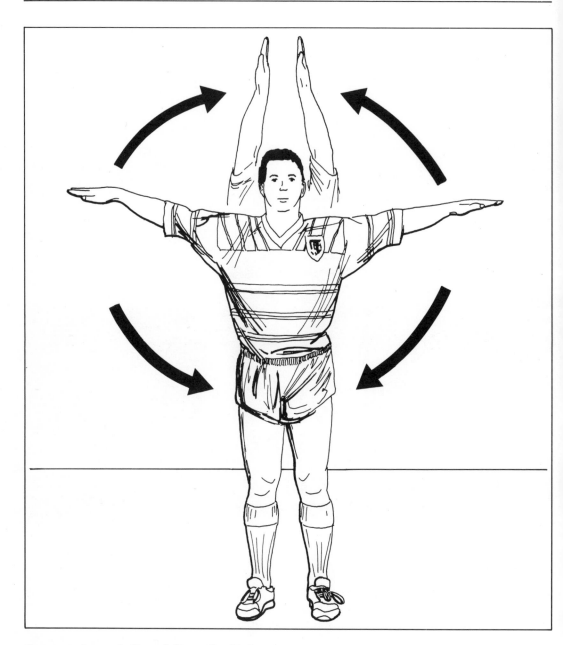

## Arm raises (shoulder girdle)

**1** Stand with feet shoulder distance apart and your arms by the sides.
**2** Raise the arms to shoulder height and then fully extend them above your head. Lower under control. Keep your head still and eyes looking forwards throughout.

# Index